Land Rover Series III

1971–85

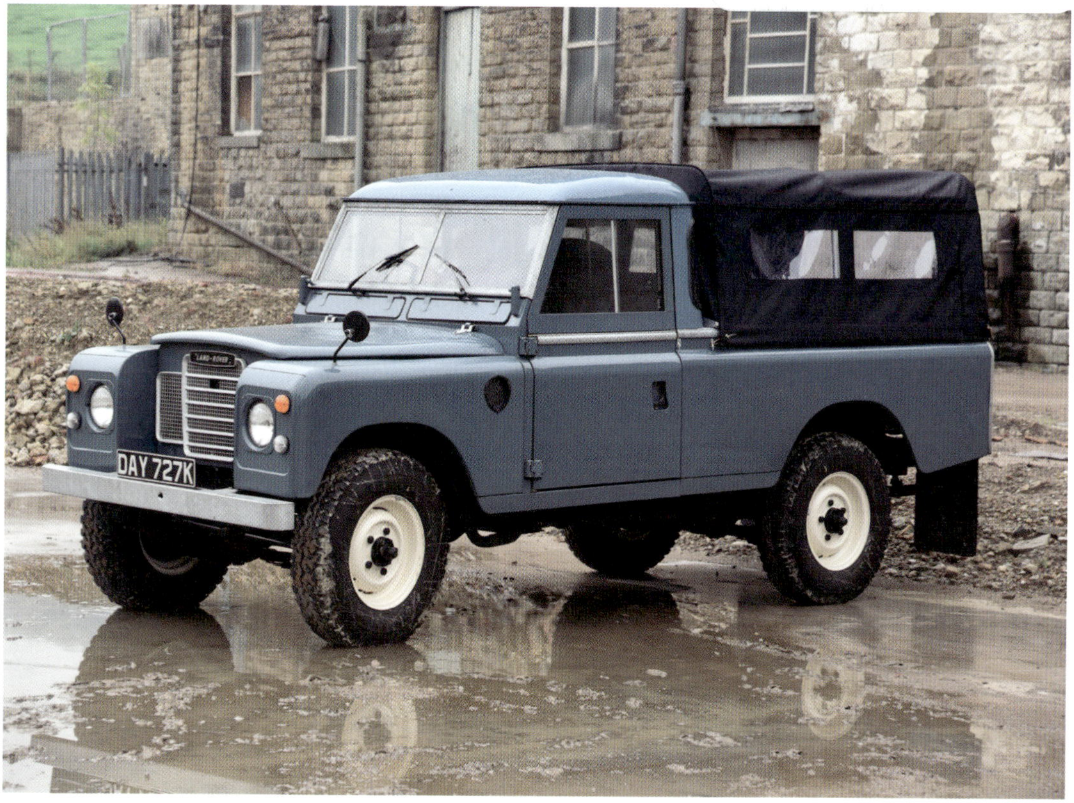

John Carroll

Key Books

CLASSIC VEHICLES SERIES, VOLUME 3

Front cover image: A 1972 Series III 88in Land Rover converted into a camper by R J Searle Ltd of Sunbury on Thames, England.

Back cover image: Three versions of the 1970s 88in Series III on an unsurfaced road in mid-Wales.

Title page image: A 1971 Series III 109in truck-cab finished in the popular factory colour of Marine Blue.

Contents page image: Eastnor Castle in Herefordshire is a recognisable landmark in many Land Rover press photos. This 1973 Series III 88in hard-top is seen in the deer park of the 19th century mock castle that is situated two miles from Ledbury.

Published by Key Books
An imprint of Key Publishing Ltd
PO Box 100
Stamford
Lincs PE19 1XQ

www.keypublishing.com

The right of John Carroll to be identified as the author of this book has been asserted in accordance with the Copyright, Designs and Patents Act 1988 Sections 77 and 78.

Copyright © John Carroll, 2021

Additional photos courtesy of Ian Clegg, Ros Woodham and Jaguar Land Rover.

The author is indebted to all the owners of the featured Land Rovers for allowing them to be photographed and for the information they have freely shared.

ISBN 978 1 913870 67 6

All rights reserved. Reproduction in whole or in part in any form whatsoever or by any means is strictly prohibited without the prior permission of the Publisher.

Typeset by SJmagic DESIGN SERVICES, India.

Contents

Introduction 4
Chapter 1 Series III 88in 1971–84 9
Chapter 2 Series III 109in 1971–85 26
Chapter 3 Series III Lightweight 1971–84 44
Chapter 4 Metalúrgica de Santa Ana SA 61
Chapter 5 Accessories 71
Chapter 6 Enthusiasts' Series IIIs 77
Chapter 7 Land Rover Clubs 89

Introduction

Hot on the heels of the 1970 introduction of the innovative and technically advanced Range Rover, a luxury 4x4 estate car, Rover sought to offer a refined version of the basic Land Rover. The new vehicle was the Series III, as an updated Series IIA, introduced in 1971 by the company that by now was a constituent part of British Leyland Motor Corporation (BLMC). In keeping with the times, and like the Range Rover, it now featured numerous plastic components.

The improvements over its Series IIA predecessor were largely cosmetic, but it was this Land Rover that would stay in production through to the 1980s. The Series III, in both 88in and 109in wheelbases, retained the body shape of the Series IIA and features such as the headlights in the wings, a feature of the last Series IIA models, but the 'at a glance' way of identifying the new model was the moulded plastic radiator grille that mimicked the shape of the wire grille on the last Series IIA models. Inside, another instant giveaway was the new plastic dashboard that replaced the centrally positioned, metal dash of earlier Land Rovers. On the Series III, the instrument cluster was moved to the driver's side on both left- and right-hand drive models.

Production of the Series III Land Rover spanned a troubled era of motor vehicle production in the UK, a time of industrial relations and managerial problems, mergers and a lack of investment in the Land Rover product. Despite this, the Series III Land Rover is the most numerous of Series Land Rovers made, as 440,000 were made over the 13-year production run, so making this the most produced model of utility Land Rover until the advent of the coil-sprung models. The Rover Company became part of the Leyland Motor Corporation (LMC) in 1967. Following this, in 1968, LMC merged with British Motor Holdings to become BLMC. Inflation and industrial relations issues added to the mix, and BLMC didn't escape unscathed; it was partly nationalised in 1975, when the UK government created a holding company called British Leyland, later to become BL, in 1978.

In 1976, midway through the Series III production run, the 1,000,000th Land Rover rolled off the Solihull, West Midlands production line. In 1980, both the petrol and diesel, four-cylinder 2.25-litre engines were upgraded with five-bearing crankshafts to increase strength. A further rationalization was the formation of the Land Rover Group (LRG), a division of BL in 1981. This brought BL's light commercial vehicle production under one management, comprising the Land Rover utility 4x4 range, the Range Rover and the Sherpa van range together. This was considered necessary as a response to the severe decline in Land

The Land Rover Series III was offered in military and civilian forms from 1971 to 1985.

Introduction

Many consider the Deep Bronze Green 88in Series III Station Wagon as the definitive Land Rover.

In truck-cab form, the 88in Series III found favour with farmers and contractors.

Rover sales – there had been a 25% decline in the period from 1980–81 for example. To redress this, some product development was considered necessary. This would ultimately lead to the coil-spring models but in the interim included new trim options to make the interior more comfortable if the buyer so wished and led to the April 1982 introduction of the 'County' specification Station Wagon Land Rovers. Series III production gradually dwindled and finally ended in 1985 once existing orders were fulfilled. In 1986, British Leyland was renamed the Rover Group in preparation for privatisation. In 1987, LRG was dismantled – the Land Rover part regaining the Rover name – and in 1988, the Rover Group was sold to British Aerospace, by which time the Ninety and One Ten models were finding buyers.

The plentiful supply of the various leaf-sprung Land Rovers made between 1948 and 1983 is largely a function of the vehicles' longevity. This has meant that, in recent years, Series Land Rovers have changed from being cheap old workhorses into desirable classics. Initially the Series Ones became sought after, and more recently the Series II/IIA and III models have gone the same way. The Series II and IIA models were made during a period that was perceived as Land Rover's golden era so, because of this, and their Vehicle Excise Duty exemption status, they now fetch a premium. Series IIIs, on the other hand, are a different story; the low mileage and one-owner examples are getting seriously expensive, but there are enough run-of-the-mill ones about to enable a bargain to be found by those looking to get into classic Land Rovers. This is especially true for those who are happy to get their hands dirty, working on their vehicle and treating it as a rolling restoration. The uninitiated think that Land Rovers last for ever, and, while there's no doubt that they last longer than many other vehicles, you need to be careful what you're going to buy. They don't really last forever, because the steel chassis and the steel bulkhead are a pair of Achilles' heels. Bear in mind that the newest Series III is now in excess of 35 years old so corrosion may be present.

Three variants of the 1970s 88in Series III on a green lane in mid-Wales.

Introduction

Many feel that because of the precarious financial position Land Rover was in when the Series III was in production, it didn't benefit from the development that it deserved. As a result, it wasn't quite up to the job asked of it on the road when supplied new, but, as the decades have slipped by, the features that limited its appeal then now endear it to the new generation of leisure buyers. Basically, as Series III Land Rovers have got older, their status in the world of Land Rover enthusiasts has evolved; back in the 1980s the newest were 'nearly new' 4x4s, and by the 1990s they were becoming 'used vehicles' and there

Land Rover Santana, SA, based in Linares, Spain, offered licence-built Series III Land Rovers.

The 109in Series III Station Wagon was popular for overland travel. This one is in Morocco.

were a few on the forecourt of every independent Land Rover garage. That has all changed now, and the Series III has taken its place in the world of cherished and classic Land Rovers. These factors mean that a Series III is, for many, a viable and charming classic car for weekend and recreational motoring where its top speed is not so crucial, while its behind-the-times interior and part-time 4x4 system can now simply be considered quaint. There are, of course, exceptions and it's still not unusual to see a Series III towing a horsebox or a livestock trailer.

Although Series III Land Rovers are now considered as 'classics', they are still suited to travelling. This mildly accessorised 1973 example is seen in Spain.

The Series III Half-Ton or Lightweight was a military version of the 88in Series III made between 1972 and 1984.

Chapter 1
Series III 88in 1971–84

By the time of the advent of the Series III in 1971, the Land Rover, in both 88in and 109in forms, was well established within Rover's range. There were some variations available: a choice of diesel or petrol engines, left and right-hand drive models, just a handful of colours and two basic body-types, the five-door Station Wagon and the two wheelbases of utility rear tub on which everything else was based. The Series III offered an amalgamation of cosmetic and engineering changes in order to modernise the Land Rover in the face of growing competition from other manufacturers, especially in export markets. Mechanically, the 2,286cc engine had its compression raised from 7:1 to 8:1, in order to increase power slightly, and this was the first Land Rover to feature synchromesh on all four gears across the range (some Series IIAs were so equipped). In 1980, both the petrol and diesel, four-cylinder 2,286cc engines were upgraded with five-bearing crankshafts to increase the engines' strength. During the Series III's production run, the full range of 88in versions offered included the three-door soft-top, three-door hard-top, two-door truck-cab pick-up and three-door Station Wagon. The choice of engines was restricted to a diesel in-line four of 2,286cc and a petrol in-line four of 2,286cc.

In keeping with 1970s trends in automotive design, both in safety and use of more advanced materials such as plastics, the simple metal dashboard of earlier models was redesigned to incorporate the new moulded plastic dash and instrument binnacle. The instrument cluster, previously centrally located, was moved to a binnacle on the driver's side. The horn and indicators were on a column stalk, instruments and switches were in front of the driver, the glovebox had a position for a radio or auxiliary gauges to be fitted and the plates for chassis number and four-wheel-drive information were on the bulkhead in front of the gear sticks. The windscreen hinges on the bulkhead were redesigned, as were the corresponding fixings on the windscreen. Although the headlights had previously been moved to the wings on late IIA models to satisfy some countries' legislation, the traditional metal radiator grille was now replaced with a plastic one. The 1,000,000th Land Rover was an 88in Series III Station Wagon made in 1976.

One of the first innovations from LRG was the introduction of new trim options to make the interior more comfortable if the buyer so wished. April 1982 saw the introduction of the 'County' specification Station Wagons, available in both 88in and 109in versions. These featured new cloth seats, soundproofing kits, tinted glass, new exterior colours and exterior graphics designed to appeal to the recreational Land Rover owner. The advent of this lifestyle-oriented County Station Wagon and the burgeoning popularity of the Camel Trophy off-road adventure were indicative of the forthcoming popularity of the 4x4 as more than simply a farmer's workhorse. Despite this, few could have foreseen the Sports Utility Vehicle (SUV) boom, the beginnings of which were still almost a decade away. For now though, the 88in wheelbase utility Land Rover with a truck-cab, a hard-top or a canvas tilt was one of the most popular variants of the Series III Land Rover range and remained popular with farmers.

The Series III, in both 88in and 109in wheelbases, retained the body shape of the Series IIA and features such as the headlights in the wings, a feature of the last Series IIA models, but the 'at a glance' way of identifying the new model was the moulded plastic radiator grille that mimicked the shape of the wire grille on the last Series IIA models.

The plastic radiator grille is the most obvious external identifier of the Series III. This Land Rover also has the optional deluxe bonnet.

Inside, another instant giveaway was the new moulded plastic dash that replaced the centrally positioned, metal dash of earlier Land Rovers. The instrument cluster was moved into a plastic binnacle in front of the driver on both left- and right-hand drive models. As well as the redesigned dashboard, new trim, such as deluxe seats, were introduced to make the interior more comfortable as an extra cost option.

By the time of the advent of the Series III in 1971, the utility hard-top in both 88in and 109in forms was well established within Land Rover's range. There were some variations available: a choice of diesel or petrol engines, left- and right-hand drive models and just a handful of colours, including Marine Blue seen on this 1977 model.

The Series III 88in took over from the Series IIA 88in and, in utility form, remained the farmer's friend, while the 88in Station Wagon continued to offer seven seats. The 88in Series III in truck-cab form was aimed at commercial users. Besides the plastic radiator grille, other details that confirm that this is a Series III include the type of bonnet hinges and the type of windscreen hinge mounts.

The three-quarter tilt was offered for both 88in and 109in models and was a canvas roof for the Land Rover's load area that fitted behind the truck-cab of models so fitted. It was popular with farmers who carried their farm dogs in the back and separate from the cab.

The Series III 88in form with a tilt roof, such as this Bronze Green 1972 example, was still officially known as the 'regular' model.

The Series III Station Wagon, now a modern classic, has sliding side windows in the sides of the hard-top and the double-skinned tropical roof panel with alpine lights and vents. Often mistakenly referred to as the 'Safari', it has roots that stretch right back to the Series One models when it was first offered in short and long wheelbase forms on 86in and 107in chassis, respectively.

The windscreen hinges and associated brackets on the Series III were of a different design to those fitted on the Series IIA and relied on a steel component welded to the front of the bulkhead. This Series III has been fitted with the door hinges and wing mirrors from a later Defender model.

The Series III 88in Station Wagon was offered with seven seats. Little changed cosmetically from the Series IIA to the Series III, although one of the most obvious changes was the use of the moulded plastic radiator grille on the latter.

The headlights were moved to the front wings on late production IIA models to comply with American, Australian and Dutch lighting regulations for export models and were retained in this position on the Series III, as seen on this 1975 model.

A 1973 seven-seater Station Wagon finished in the popular combination of Marine Blue with a contrasting Limestone tropical roof panel. Station Wagons were fitted with a side-hung rear door rather than top and bottom tailgates, to allow easy access and egress for rear-seat passengers.

This 1982 Station Wagon is from the later end of the Series III production run but is largely unchanged. Additionally, it has period accessories in the form of freewheeling hubs and towing eyes fitted, while its door mirrors are the later Defender type.

Launched in August 1981 as a 1982, and new to the Land Rover range, was the Land Rover County Station Wagon in 88in and 109in forms. The 88in is seen here, but both models had fabric upholstery and other features that enhanced the interior. Externally, county stripes were applied to the bold colours used, including red and a dark brown known as Russet Brown. This was also used on other BL cars of the era, and the idea of a luxury Land Rover caught on, to the extent that County Station Wagon became a recognised interior spec for the duration of the later 90 and 110 production runs. This is a 1984 model where the rear windows and rear light arrangement varies from the earlier Station Wagons.

A 1973 Series III 88in hard-top on an unsurfaced road in Mid Wales. The vehicle's ability off-road was unquestioned because of its short wheelbase and high ground clearance that contribute to a steep ramp break over angle. This asset was abetted by correspondingly steep approach and departure angles.

This 1982-registered 1983 model 88in hard-top is finished in one of the less common colours for the range, Pastel Green, and has the side repeater indicators that were fitted to later Series III models.

This County Station Wagon that has been converted into a vehicle with a full-tilt roof shows how the Land Rover's Meccano-like construction means that large components can be simply unbolted and how the hood sticks for the canvas soft-top roof are substituted using the same mounting holes.

The same vehicle with its canvas tilt in place. Only the County Station Wagon's distinctive colour and adhesive graphics suggest that it was ever anything other than an 88in 'Regular' Land Rover.

Land Rover campers are generally based on LWB models because of their larger internal space, but an exception is the Searle Safari Sleeper, a camper conversion made by Searle of Sunbury on Thames. The company's conversion provided basic sleeping accommodation in an 88in Land Rover and used an unusual combination of a tropical roof panel, blind sides and rear door to enhance privacy but allow light into the sleeping area.

In order to create bed space in the Searle-converted 88in Series III, the rear bulkhead is cut away and a removable rail fitted to support the front seats. When preparing the vehicle for sleeping, the rear-seat bases are moved together, the support rail is removed and the front seats are folded forwards. The gaps are filled with the backs of the rear seats, and the resulting flat area equates to a double bed.

Land Rover fire appliances are also generally based on LWB models that offer a larger rear load area for pumps and other firefighting equipment, but this one is based on an 88in diesel hard-top. A ladder rack is one of the few external modifications. The 1982 model was used by Merseyside Fire Brigade and stationed at West Kirby on the Wirral in North West England.

The popularity of the Series III led to many owners accessorising them to some extent. This late-model Series III Station Wagon has been fitted with freewheeling hubs on the front axle and later-type Defender mirrors, both of which modifications are popular for Land Rovers of this age. Additionally, it has been fitted with aftermarket white eight-spoke wheels and radial tyres.

This 1975 Station Wagon, seen on an unsurfaced road, also has the same sort of modifications, namely freewheeling hubs on the front axle, later-type Defender mirrors and aftermarket 15in white eight-spoke wheels and radial tyres.

Against the uncertain background of the Troubles in Northern Ireland, the British military purchased Land Rovers that it then referred to as Series 3 rather than III and did not reclassify as Rover Mk 12s. Because the Lightweight was in widespread use, relatively few of the normal 88in models were purchased for military use. Those that were acquired were, in the main, Commercial Logistics (CL) models in Station Wagon, hard-top and tilt versions.

A 1980 88in and a 1978 109in Series III Station Wagon finished in Marine Blue with Limestone tropical roofs parade in the sunshine at a Land Rover enthusiasts' event.

That Series III Land Rovers were capable off-road was unquestioned, but it was subsequently proven on the world stage when the Series III was chosen as the transport for the Camel Trophy, a competitive, international off-road adventure. In the twilight years of Series III production, the 1983 Camel Trophy went to the Republic of Zaire (now Democratic Republic of the Congo) in Africa.

The competing teams from seven countries used diesel-powered 88in Station Wagons, while the organisers relied on 109ins on the journey from the capital, Kinshasa, to Kisangani. The vehicles were equipped with roof racks, winches, bridging ladders and jerrycans but were mechanically standard. These replica vehicles have been accurately recreated to portray the 1983 Portuguese team vehicle.

This working Series III hard-top doubles as a colourful advert for its owner's business, the Strawberry Field Pancake Cottage in Blackwater, Kenmare, Ireland. It is located on a minor road on the famous Ring of Kerry overlooking the Slievaduff Valley, an area that is a favourite with tourists and locals alike.

In 1981, Land Rover built four prototype 88in Stage One V8s. All were based on modified Series III chassis that were numbered consecutively within the Series III production sequence. Two were completed as utility models and two as Station Wagons. This is one of the latter, and its sister vehicle is also in the Dunsfold Collection of Land Rovers and both have recently been restored.

Like the more numerous 109in counterparts, the Stage One V8 88in carries a V8 decal on its bodywork.

Inevitably, because of their useful mix of being both a classic and useful, Series III Land Rovers have found favour with Land Rover club members as this picture of a pair of Marine Blue 88ins being driven on an unsurfaced Mid Wales green lane demonstrates.

On rough tracks, the axles and suspension need to articulate to allow the vehicle to cross uneven ground. Once a wheel leaves the ground after maximum articulation is achieved, drive to that wheel, and therefore that axle (where standard differentials are fitted), can cause the vehicle to become stuck, although in this situation the downhill slope will allow the vehicle to continue forwards with drive from the front axle.

When a wheel on each axle leaves the ground, drive is lost to both axles, and the vehicle becomes stuck, it is described as being 'cross axled'. Here, this Land Rover still has drive to the rear axle, so isn't quite stuck. In some cases, when stuck, turning the steering wheel allows a front wheel to regain traction if it touches the ground.

Many unmaintained tracks and roads resemble stream beds because the rainfall washes away the soil and small stones, leaving the larger stones without any covering or infill. Such a track provides no insurmountable obstacles for this 1980 Series III, especially as it is fitted with aftermarket off-road tyres.

A rocky road but a road nonetheless, and the civilian model 2,286cc petrol-engined Series III 88in with its retrofitted tilt and tailgate is seen following a Series III Lightweight of similar vintage along this famous road in Mid Wales known as Strata Florida (Ystrad Fflur).

Chapter 2
Series III 109in 1971–85

LWB Series III Land Rovers were, with the exception of the Station Wagon models, simply longer versions of the 88in models. However, they had slightly different rear spring arrangements, heavier duty springs and a third engine option. Besides the in-line four-cylinder, 2,286cc petrol and diesel engines was the option of an in-line, six-cylinder, petrol engine that displaced 2,625cc. The LWB Series III vehicles also had a heavier duty Dana 'Salisbury' unit fitted for increased strength to solve the problem of the rear axle half-shafts breaking, so the vehicle could cope with heavier loads.

There was also a Series III version of the One Ton model produced until 1977. As the Series IIA version, it was basically a Series IIB Forward Control built with a standard bonneted 109in body. It had a six-cylinder 2.6-litre, petrol engine, a lower ratio gearbox, Salisbury front and rear axles and 9.00x16 tyres. The chassis was unique to the model. These Land Rovers were commonly used by utility companies but fewer than 300 were built.

The Series III 109in Station Wagon was offered with a choice of either ten or 12 seats and little changed cosmetically from the Series IIA to the Series III. As on the 88in models, the most obvious external change was the use of the moulded plastic radiator grille. The headlights had already moved to the front wings on late production Series IIA models to comply with American, Australian and Dutch lighting regulations for export models and were retained in this position on the Series III. New trim options, such as deluxe seats, were introduced to make the interior more comfortable as an extra cost option. These changes led to the introduction of the 109in 'County' specification Station Wagon in April 1982. These had all-new cloth seats taken from a Leyland lorry and other options designed to appeal to the family user or caravanner.

Each generation of overlander uses a different generation of Land Rover for its journeys and, for a period, the Series III 109in was the definitive vehicle for overland travel. The 109in, particularly in three-door hard-top and five-door Station Wagon forms was the vehicle of choice for the 'hippy trail' trips overland to India and journeys across the Sahara by way of Tamanrasset. Of course, many of those trips faithfully recorded in people's photo albums were made more than 30 years ago when the Series III was still a relatively new Land Rover and the roof tent was a fad that hadn't yet arrived. Taking a Series III to India or Africa now is a completely different proposition because the journey has to be made in a Land Rover that is now considered as a classic.

With hindsight, it can be seen that the Stage Ones – officially the 109 V8 – introduced in 1979 were an attempt to modernise the 109in Series III models for the 1980s. They were intended to compete with Japanese manufacturers that were making significant in-roads in Land Rover's export markets. The Stage One V8 was offered in truck-cab, blind hard-top and 10 and 12-seater Station Wagons. Bright colours were perceived as modern and included as options in addition to the standard Series III colours, Java Green, Masai Red, Inca Yellow and Pageant Blue. In 1982, Russet Brown was added to the list of optional colours. It may have been the paint that caught the eye, but it was underneath that the serious changes had been made.

The Stage One V8 had a version of the Rover V8 under the bonnet. It was the 3,528cc unit from the Range Rover and came with the Range Rover's manual LT95 gearbox, diff-lock and two-speed transfer box as well. This made it permanent four-wheel-drive, although, in contrast to the Range Rover, its axles were leaf-sprung but featured the Range Rover 3.54:1 differential ratio. The rear axle was the proven Salisbury unit. The increase in power was deemed necessary to compete with Toyota's in-line, six-cylinder Land Cruiser in much of Australia and Africa. To fit the Rover V8 engine and gearbox, the Series III 109in chassis was modified, including having its front crossmember repositioned further forwards. Also moved further forward was the radiator grille, and this became a point of debate for many Land Rover enthusiasts. The flush front of the Stage One looked modern and created room for the V8, but, arguably, isn't pretty and conflicts with the remainder of the vehicle's traditional 'Series-look'. Production of Stage Ones ran from 1979 until 1983, and many, including the entire first year's production, were permanently exported while sales of the thirstier V8 model were low in the UK. The production run of this stopgap model was short, as it would soon be superseded by the One Ten and a further year later, the Ninety.

A further variation on the 109in theme was the introduction of the High Capacity Pick-Up (HCPU) in April 1982. This was a pick-up truck with a load bed that offered considerably more capacity than the standard truck-cab pick-up. It was offered in response to the growing popularity of other makers' 4x4 pick-ups – notably Toyota – around the world. The HCPU was offered in four-cylinder and Stage One V8 forms and became popular with public utility companies and other commercial users. Later, the model survived the transition to coil springs and would remain in production until the cessation of Defender production in 2016.

A 1971 109in truck-cab with its spare wheel mounted in the side of the load bed. A galvanized box is fitted to the wheel box to allow the wheel to sit low, and the retaining bracket is mounted to the inside of the body's galvanized capping.

Possibly because they were used as working vehicles and worn out, few 109in truck-cab models have been restored. Therefore, this pristine 1973 Marine Blue example seen at a classic car event is now quite a rare Land Rover.

The long wheelbase Series III vehicles had slightly different rear spring arrangements and heavier duty springs to the SWB models and had a heavier duty 'Salisbury' rear axle as standard to cope with heavier loads. This example has the wider Forward Control-type wheels fitted.

Numerous accessories were offered for Series III Land Rovers. This 1979 Station Wagon has been equipped with headlamp guards, recovery eyes and a capstan winch.

The Series III was the most numerous of the Series Land Rover models, and both 88in and 109in models were offered as truck-cabs (pick-ups), hard-tops, soft-tops and Station Wagons. The 109in Station Wagon continued to use a different body to the hard- and soft-top models, to enable the fitting of the second pair of doors.

The exterior revisions to the Series III included redesigned door hinges and retained the revised headlamp layout introduced earlier but incorporated the new plastic radiator grille. Changes were also made to the interior where the fascia received some crash padding, and a plastic instrument binnacle was positioned in front of the driver and contained improved heater controls.

This left-hand drive 1985 Series III Station Wagon is one of the last manufactured. By 1985, the One Ten Station Wagon had been in production for two years and offered the same five-door body configuration.

The Series III 109in Station Wagon was offered with a choice of either ten or 12 seats. Little changed cosmetically from the Series IIA to the Series III, one of the most obvious changes, of course, was the use of the moulded plastic radiator grille – seen here – on the latter.

The Series III featured sealed beam headlamps mounted in the wings, surrounded by a square trim that superseded the chrome trim rings on some earlier models. They were screwed into place, which enabled access for a screwdriver through grooves in the trim to adjust the lamps' alignment. Side and indicator lights are separate circular units.

This Portuguese-registered 109in hard-top has a roof that comprises a tropical roof panel fixed to sides that incorporate fixed side windows. These are often referred to as 'export windows' because a hard-top so equipped in the UK would have attracted Purchase Tax, making the vehicle more expensive than one with blind sides.

The 109in Station Wagon was popular for overland trips and with companies offering such trips as paid-for holidays. This 1980 109in model was fitted with blind rear side panels and painted to resemble the vehicles that starred in the 1960s TV series *Daktari* and used for a trip to Morocco as recently as 2015.

The 109in hard-top was often used as a commercial vehicle, as evidenced by this 1981 model sign written with the name of a haulage company. The working 109in hard-top was still an important part of the Land Rover line up in the 1980s, but it was now facing imported 4x4 competition from vehicles such as the Toyota Hilux.

Another new model intended to compete with other commercial 4x4 manufacturers around the world was the High Capacity Pick-Up (HCPU). This was the ninth body-type available across the civilian Land Rover range and was a pick-up truck with an oversize load bed that offered more carrying capacity than the standard LWB pick-up model. Its bigger loadspace and corresponding rear tailgate were wider, meaning that standard pallets could be loaded into it with a forklift.

The Stage One V8 – officially the 109 V8 – was an attempt to modernise the 109in Series III models for the 1980s, something that was necessary to compete with Japanese manufacturers who were making inroads into important export markets. The interim solution was to develop the extant Series III 109in and fit the 3,500cc Rover V8 engine and the Range Rover four-speed gearbox. This boosted the vehicle's power and incorporated a better gearbox.

The 109in V8 vehicles, including Station Wagons, were the first utility Land Rovers with permanent four-wheel-drive, while the need to move the radiator forwards to make room for the V8 engine resulted in the flat-fronted appearance that became ubiquitous with the Ninety and One Ten models soon afterwards. Bright colours were perceived as modern and included, as options on top of the standard Series III colours, Java Green, Masai Red, Inca Yellow and Pageant Blue. Production of Stage Ones ran only from 1979 to 1983.

As the 109 V8 was intended to be the first stage of Land Rover's recovery plan, it became generally known as the Stage One V8 and had Land Rover V8 decals on its rear quarter panels.

The styling of the Stage One V8 perhaps reflects the hybrid nature of the vehicle. It is very much a leaf-sprung Series III 109in but with a bonnet and grille that, in order to accommodate the V8 engine and full-time 4x4 system from the Range Rover, foreshadowed those later fitted to the coil spring models.

The 109in Land Rover was often the basis for fire appliances such as this 1975, 2,625cc, six-cylinder model converted by Branbridge Fire and Security Equipment Ltd. It is the Branbridge Mk I version with a three-person cab and the specially designed low-height fire tender body. The front bumper has been replaced with a water tank that ensures the vehicle's centre of gravity remains low. This vehicle was supplied to the Wellcome Foundation on 1 December 1975. Subsequently, the Branbridge company was acquired by Pilcher-Greene Ltd.

Many Land Rover-based fire appliances, such as this 1975, petrol 2,286cc 109in, are designated as Light Four-Wheel-Drive Pumps (L4P) and are a smaller version of the frontline fire engine. Deployed in rural locations, they can negotiate difficult terrain, cope with narrow streets and use in remote areas. This machine, based on a 109in hard-top and fitted with a Godiva Vehicle-Mounted Pump, was originally in service with Hampshire Fire Brigade and was based at Fordingbridge.

HCB-Angus was founded in 1933 and produced numerous fire appliances in its Totton, Southampton factory for fire services in the UK and abroad. This 1980 109in Land Rover L4P was one such machine, and the conversion was based on the petrol 2,286cc chassis cab model. It was supplied new to the County of Clwyd fire service in North Wales and based in Llangollen.

This HCB-Angus appliance features an especially constructed rear body that features side lockers and carries a 100-gallon water tank and a rear-mounted Godiva pump and first-aid hose reel. Its roof rack carries two lengths of suction hose with baskets that enabled water to be extracted from rivers or ponds.

The length and proportions of the 109in wheelbase Land Rover meant that it was ideal for the fitting of numerous specialist rear bodies. Companies such as Pilcher-Green, Marshalls and Glover Webb built bodies for ambulances and campers. This conversion, based on a six-cylinder, 2,625cc 109in, was built as a mobile laboratory for testing fuel and has been converted into a camper.

The advantage of the 109in hard-top over the equivalent 88in for conversion to campers was that it offered a considerably larger rear loadspace and had a bigger payload because of heavier springs and larger wheels and tyres. The Searle Carawagon camper conversion to the 109in three-door Land Rover was initially manufactured when the Series IIA was in production. It remained largely unaltered when based on the Series III – such as the 1973 'Desert Rat' pictured – and retained its factory-approved status.

A less numerous 109in Carawagon camper conversion was this, based on the five-door Station Wagon. This is a 1972 model and has the same elevating roof arrangement but features a different internal layout. Three-door models were known as the Carawagon Deluxe, and five-doors as the Carawagon Ultimate.

By the time the Series III Land Rover was in production, Carawagon badging was more evident on the proprietary Searle Carawagon camper conversions than previously, as this grille badge demonstrates.

The Carawagon Deluxe was a 109in comprehensively equipped as a camper with beds and bunks for four, a cooker, table, in-built storage facilities and an elevating roof. It also had an awning rail that could be pulled out from the roof panel over the rear door to support a rear tent. Here the roof is lowered and the vehicle is in travel mode.

The British Army had numerous specialised Land Rovers including Tactical Command Posts (TCP), armoured cars, fire engines and ambulances. TCP was the designation given to these 109in Carawagon Land Rovers converted into dual purpose office/sleeping accommodation for senior officers by Carawagon, formerly Searle International of Sunbury on Thames. The TCPs were based on Series III 109in hard-tops with Carawagon's unique roof conversion.

A TCP with its roof folded away. This variant of the military 109in was fitted with a roof rack over the cab that enabled the elevating portion of the roof to be raised and lowered. It was used to carry camouflage netting and similar equipment.

The TCP was deployed when a senior officer needed to command operations in forward operating areas. It used a rear 9x9 tent to increase its interior space for communications purposes.

The TCP 109ins were painted in standard British Army camouflage colours. The matt green and matt black combination was applied to those vehicles deployed in Europe as part of the British Army of the Rhine (BAOR). The military Carawagon roofs did not include skylights like the civilian camper models.

 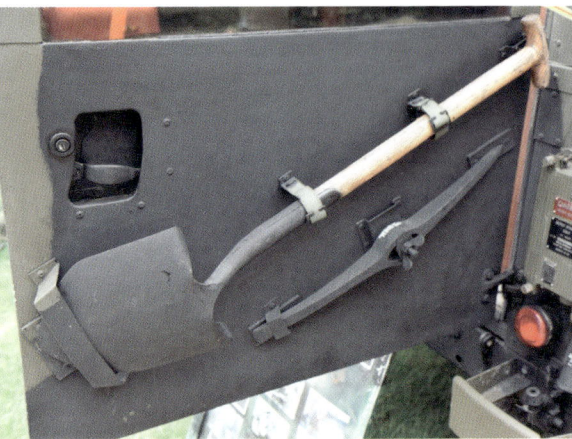

Rather than a straightforward camper conversion, the TCP models were equipped as offices with radio communication equipment to enable commands to be passed to deployed units and soldiers. This Land Rover enthusiast's vehicle has been painstakingly equipped to recreate such a setting, with radios, maps and a dummy officer. The office desk works like the table in the camper version in that it is a cupboard door that slides into the cupboard horizontally to create a workspace.

The TCP Carawagons had a rear door rather than a tailgate but the standard military pioneer tools – a Bulldog shovel and a pickaxe – were still fitted to the vehicle in the standard mounting brackets.

The 109in Land Rover was supplied in two versions to the British Army, and both were powered by 2,286cc petrol engines, but there were 24-volt Fitted For Radio (FFR) and 12-volt General Service (GS) models. A further variation was that the Army ordered batches of both left- and right-hand drive models. The LHD models were largely used in BAOR roles in Europe, while the RHD ones were used in the UK, including the 30+ year Operation *Banner* deployment to Northern Ireland. Pictured is a RHD 24-volt FFR model made in 1984.

The Army's policy of selling its used Land Rovers on a rotational basis meant that numerous ex-military Land Rovers found civilian enthusiast owners. In exactly the same way that civilian 109ins were the basis of camper conversions, many military ones were the basis for home conversions. This 1979 example has been fitted with a hard-top roof and a roof rack that carries a roof tent.

At some point, the same vehicle was repainted to reflect its military history but still offer its owners a convenient and comfortable place to camp at historic vehicle rallies.

This ex-military 109in was manufactured in 1977 and has been repurposed for work use following its disposal by the Army. Its canvas tilt has been replaced by a previously used truck-cab roof and its load bed fitted with a hydraulic platform manufactured by Simon Engineering, which means the vehicle can help workers access the exterior of high buildings for maintenance purposes.

Chapter 3
Series III Lightweight 1971–84

During the production run of the military 88in Lightweight, the civilian Series IIA models became the Series III. As a result, from 1971 onwards, Series III Lightweights were constructed to fulfil military contracts. The nature of the Lightweight and its use within NATO meant that batches of Lightweights were sold to other nations' armies, notably Holland. The use of the Lightweight as a standard British Army Land Rover meant that it served across the British Army in general service and specialist roles.

The Series IIA 88in 'Half-Ton' or Lightweight of 1968–71 – confusingly designated the Rover 1 – was the result of meeting the British Army's requirement for an air-portable vehicle. The limiting factor was the size and payloads of the aircraft then in service. Existing 88in models were too wide to be carried two-abreast in the transport aircraft of the mid-1960s, and they were too heavy to be carried singly underslung on the military helicopters then in service. The Lightweight was therefore developed on the existing 88in chassis but incorporating a narrower body to meet the first requirement. To meet the second, the body comprised demountable sections, so that the basic drivable vehicle could be heli-lifted without its less vital body sections, such as doors, upper rear panels, roof, windscreen and bumper, and the still drivable vehicle was within the payload of the then in-service helicopters. The result was a distinctive-looking, angular-shaped vehicle with its flat-panelled bodywork and even more so when stripped of its doors, windscreen and upper bodywork. In its built-up form, it was actually heavier than the vehicle it was derived from, and soon new transport aircraft and new helicopters, which entered service in the mid-1960s, made both of the original design requirements redundant. However, the Army was impressed with the basic, stripped-down design of the Lightweight and standardised it as its short wheelbase Land Rover in both LHD and RHD forms. All the early Lightweights had headlamps mounted in the grille panel in a manner similar to regular Series IIA models, but after almost 3,000 were made, from 1969 onwards, the headlamps were repositioned in the wings.

The second-generation model of the Half-Ton, the Series III, entered production in April 1972, some eight months after production of the Series III civilian models had begun. This was because the Solihull factory had to complete outstanding orders for the Series IIA version. Series III Half-Tons looked very much like the Series IIA models they replaced, but changes included a key rather than push-button start, a Smiths heater, modified upper bulkhead and windscreen hinges, the latest all-synchromesh gearbox and a larger (9.5in diameter) clutch plate. The 12-volt models had an alternator in place of the earlier dynamo. All vehicles retained the earlier style of instrument panel and did not switch to the civilian Series III type; column switchgear was, however, the civilian Series III type. From 1980 onwards, the wing mirrors were relocated to the doors, and rear fog lights were added.

In British use there were essentially four versions of the Lightweight: left- and right-hand drive and 12- and 24-volt versions. The vehicles were delivered as General Service (GS) (12-volt) or Fitted For Radio (FFR) (24-volt) variants. All British military versions had the four-cylinder, 2,286cc petrol engine, but diesel models were supplied to the Dutch and Danish militaries from 1976. The use of the Lightweight as a standard British Army Land Rover meant that it served across the British Army and the RAF in GS, FFR and specialist roles. Lightweights were prepared for air transport, helicopter delivery, amphibious landings, winterised for use in Norway on NATO's northern flank, modified for weapons-carrying functions as well as ceremonial duties, and many were fitted with a Vehicle Protection Kit (VPK) for service in Ulster. The so-called 'Troubles' in Northern Ireland were a drain on military resources and, at their height in 1972, there were 27,000 British military personnel based in Northern Ireland. It was against such an uncertain background that the British military purchased Land Rovers, which it referred to as Series 3 rather than III. Because the Lightweight was in widespread use, relatively few of the normal 88in models were purchased for military use.

Lightweights were supplied from the factory with full-tilt canvas roofs, although some were converted by their military users into hard-tops and Station Wagons, using modified civilian panels. Going 'full tilt' in British usage tends to mean going at full speed or force, but in Land Rover terms it's the name for a canvas roof of the whole vehicle, from the top of the windscreen frame to the rear of the body tub. In other Land Rover applications there are three-quarter tilts that fit behind truck-cabs as well as numerous other variations such as aftermarket canvas truck-cabs, tonneau covers and bikini-top roofs. The origin of the word 'tilt' as a canopy for a wagon, boat, or stall – meaning a cover of coarse cloth or canvas – is said to originate from ancient English words such as *teld* or *telte*, which are similar to the old German *zelt* and old Norse *tjald*. It is believed to have originated in the 15th century but has endured to the 21st century when classic 4x4s and military lorries tend to be some of the few vehicles still so equipped.

The final Lightweight models were built in 1984–85 and entered British military service early the following year. They were still in service when the Berlin Wall came down in November 1989 and the epoch referred to as The Cold War ended with the collapse of the Soviet Union in 1991, and some would deploy to the Gulf in the same year.

The Series III version of the Half-Ton military Land Rover, or Lightweight, entered production in April 1972, some eight months after production of the Series III civilian models had begun. This was because the Solihull factory first had to complete outstanding orders for the Series IIA version. The Series III Half-Tons, officially the Truck, Utility, General Service, 1/2 Ton, 4x4, Rover Series 3, looked very much like the Series IIA models they replaced.

A 1983 Series III Half-Ton, or Lightweight, Land Rover, in its basic military form. It is in its complete 'built-up' form here, but the front bumper, windscreen, bulkhead top section, spare-wheel doors, rear tub top section, split tailgate, canvas tilt and its hood sticks can all be removed to make the vehicle lighter for airlifting.

The Series III Lightweights had their headlamps in the wings and a one-piece wire radiator grille that were carried over from the late Series IIA models. The top section of the bulkhead has Series III-type hinges for the windscreen, while its lights are of the standard UK-specification military type.

Above: The late-model Lightweights, like this 1983 model, were fitted with the plastic version of Land Rover's trademark oval badge.

Right: The spare wheel and tyre is carried on the bonnet in the manner of many civilian Land Rovers but is held in place by three straps that link to a metal ring and hook to loops bolted to the bonnet.

Below: The military Lightweight carried pioneer tools in the form of a Bulldog shovel and a pickaxe with a removable shaft, on the top portion of the two-piece tailgate. They are held in place with a combination of webbing straps and brackets incorporated into the tailgate hinges.

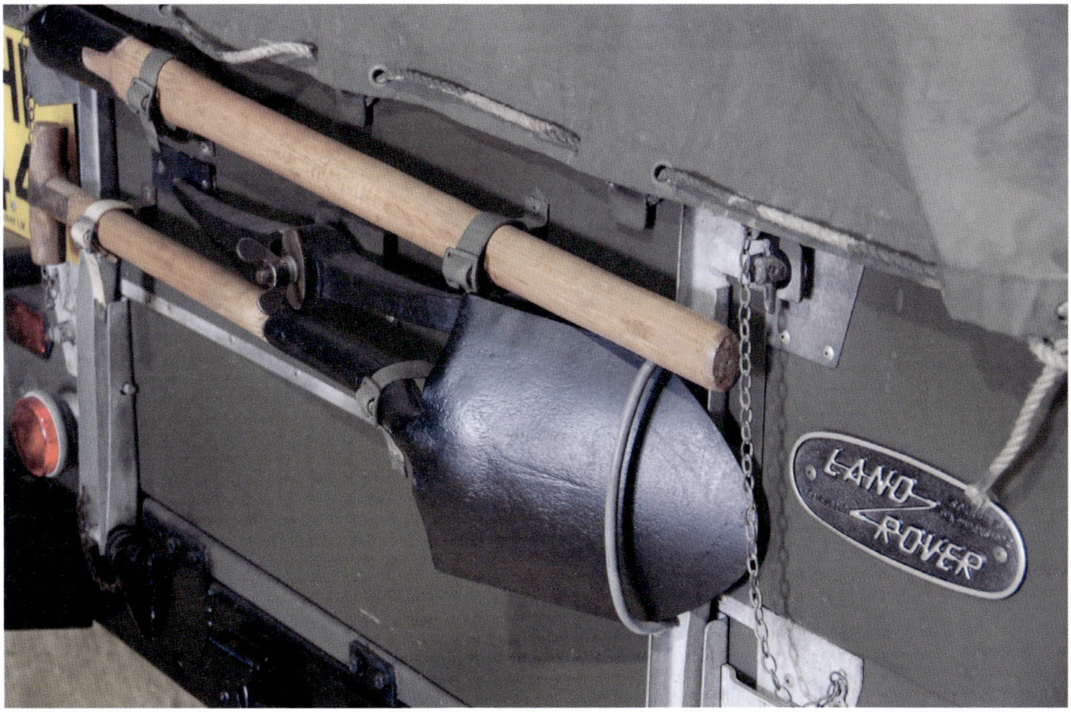

This Series III Lightweight was supplied to the British Army under a contract of 1973–74 for a batch of more than 860 FFR Half-Tons and has been restored to its original specification, including aerials.

This Series III Lightweight was one of a batch supplied to the British Army in 1980–81 under a contract for more than 500 FFR Half-Tons and remains in its original configuration.

This Lightweight is finished in the unusual Cold War-era Berlin Brigade urban camouflage that dates back to 1982. The block scheme was designed by the Officer Commanding the 4/7 Royal Dragoon Guards tank squadron to disguise the shape of tanks in the city's urban areas. The urban colours, a combination of white, blue-grey and brown, were successful and adopted by all British Forces in Berlin.

The RAF also used Series III Lightweight Land Rovers procured under a series of contracts issued between 1972 and 1980. Most were GS models, although there were LHD and RHD vehicles ordered. They were supplied painted in the same shade of RAF Blue Grey as this 1980 model, which is one of a batch of 125 GS models. Apart from their colour, the RAF GS Lightweights were the same as army models with a 12-volt electrical system and a 2,286cc four-cylinder petrol engine. This example retains its original military bumper with bumperettes and bridging plate fixed to the grille.

By 1980, fog lights were mandatory for motor vehicles in the UK, so this Land Rover was fitted with the additional circular lights either side of the tailgate. It also features the pioneer tools on the two-piece tailgate and a NATO tow hitch, although the drop plate and 50mm ball below it is a later addition.

Many RAF Lightweights were resprayed NATO green while in service, with the addition of a yellow flash for airfield use as is the case with this 1979 Land Rover.

Some Lightweights used on airfields were painted yellow so that they were visible to arriving and departing aircraft for safety reasons. This GS model was supplied to the RAF under a 1983 Tri-Service contract, which meant the vehicles could have been allocated to any of the services.

This 1980 Lightweight is a 24-volt FFR model restored with its radio equipment and radio operator's seat in its rear load bed and the colours of the Royal Military Police.

This basic RHD GS Lightweight is a 1972 model, which means that it is from early on in the production run of Series III Half-Tons. Visible above its front bumper are the lifting eyes that facilitated lifting by helicopters and aboard ships by cranes.

This 1974 Lightweight is an RHD FFR model and has shackles in its front lifting eyes as well as a NATO tow hitch fitted to the bumper, which is pre-drilled for such a component and allows it to be fitted and still provide access to the starting handle hole (seen to the right of the tow hitch).

The Lightweight Land Rover is popular with military vehicle enthusiasts, as it was a practical and bona fide military vehicle that was not offered for civilian sales until disposed of second-hand by the military forces. This nicely presented 1974 model is seen at a military vehicle show.

A GS model Lightweight that was supplied under a 1979 contract and is restored in sand paint. Lightweights and other Land Rovers of the same age were deployed during the first Gulf War of 1990–91.

The horizontal line below the Union Flag sticker is the joint where the top section of the rear tub lifts off and where the two-piece tailgate divides when the Lightweight is being stripped for heli-lifting.

The Lightweight was frequently fitted with 6.50x16 Goodyear Xtragrip tyres, and the spare was carried on the bonnet and strapped in place so that it could be removed if the vehicle was to be airlifted.

The Lightweight's box section rear crossmember, an integral part of the vehicle's chassis, is supplied with pre-drilled holes that contain steel tubes to prevent the box section being crushed, for the standard NATO tow hitch that facilitated the towing of Sankey trailers.

A 1980 RHD GS Lightweight photographed on a chalky section of the Ridgeway, an ancient highway that extends through Wiltshire and Berkshire.

A 1983 GS Lightweight (left) and a 1979 FFR model being exhibited at an enthusiasts' Land Rover event at the British Motor Museum at Gaydon in Warwickshire.

This RHD is a 1984 model from one of the last batches of Lightweights made and ordered under a Tri-Service contract.

An RHD Lightweight parading at a military vehicle enthusiasts' event, with its matching Sankey trailer. The Sankey trailer was so-called because it was supplied by the manufacturer, Joseph Sankey and Sons Ltd of Wellington, Shropshire, a metal pressings company.

The Sankey trailer is of pressed-steel welded frame construction with semi-elliptic suspension mounted on a tubular axle. Brakes on both wheels are actuated by an overrun mechanism from the draught eye. An all-steel cargo body is fitted that incorporates wheel valances, a duckboard floor and a canopy to protect the load. Standard electrical equipment and warning triangles are also fitted.

Later variants of the Sankey trailer, such as this one seen with its 1980 Series III Lightweight tug, had a drop-down tailgate to facilitate easier loading.

This Lightweight Gunship was a trials vehicle for the Dutch Army that comprised a standard Lightweight Land Rover and an M40A1 recoilless rifle. This conversion was carried out by Marshalls of Cambridge and is unique, as no others were built, because orders for the gunship were not forthcoming.

A Series III Lightweight in United Nations and Royal Marines Commando markings set up in a diorama in the Ex-Military Military Land Rover Association's display at a Land Rover enthusiasts' event.

An RHD FFR Lightweight that was supplied to the Army under a 1979 contract for around 350 vehicles on display at a Land Rover show. It has been painstakingly restored with military radio aerials and is finished in the matt green and matt black camouflage paintwork that vehicles deployed in Europe used.

The Lightweight Land Rover Club was founded in 1990 and is a member of the Association of Land Rover Clubs. It welcomes owners of all types of Lightweight, whether modified or standard. Here, a group of members from the club, in seven Lightweights, visit the battlefields of the Somme.

Ex-military Lightweight Land Rovers suit being upgraded as civilian Land Rovers. This LHD Portuguese one belongs to a restaurant owner in Porto. It is finished in satin black pair and has subtle upgrades including Series III deluxe seats and upgraded towing eyes. In this guise, it is ideal transport for a sunny seaside resort location.

The Lightweight Land Rover celebrated its 50th anniversary in 2019, and one of the events to mark the occasion was a large gathering of Lightweights at the long-running military vehicle show in Kent known as the War and Peace Revival Show.

Chapter 4
Metalúrgica de Santa Ana SA

The history of Metalúrgica de Santa Ana SA, a Spanish automobile manufacturer based in Linares, in the province of Jaén, Spain, and how it came to manufacture Land Rovers in General Franco's Spain is worth delving into. The company had originally been founded to manufacture agricultural equipment with support from the Spanish government, which wanted local businesses to encourage development in the Andalucía region of southern Spain. Metalúrgica de Santa Ana SA entered into talks with the Rover Company in 1956 in an attempt to get a licensing agreement to build Land Rover Series models in its factory, in a similar way to the Minerva company in Belgium, Tempo in Germany and Morattab company in Iran, which all built Series Land Rovers under licence. Agreement was reached and production of Complete Knocked Down (CKD) kits began in 1958. Soon afterwards, in 1962, the company became responsible for promoting the Santana and Land Rover brands in the Central and South American markets as well as parts of Africa, and CKD kits were supplied to Moroccan and Costa Rican customers.

In the late 1960s, Santana also produced military vehicles developed in Linares for the Spanish, Moroccan and Egyptian militaries. Known as the 'Militar', these 4x4s, in 88in and 109in wheelbase forms, were similar to the British Land Rover Lightweight. The model was basically a re-bodied Series III designed for helicopter lifting and was no narrower than an 88in or 109in. They had load capacities of a quarter and one tonne for the 88in and 109in respectively and featured canvas tilts. Numerous specialised military versions including armoured and ambulance were developed.

From 1968 onwards, Santana began to develop its own versions of the Land Rover Series models, developing new engines and new models, and this led to a change of name from Land Rover Santana, SA to Santana, by which time the Spanish-made vehicles comprised 100% of locally manufactured components, and almost 250,000 Land Rovers had been produced. Sequentially, the Santana versions of the Series III were the Santana Series III of 1974–78, the Santana Series III of 1978–83 (an evolved version of the Land Rover Series III), the Santana Series IIIA of 1983–87 and the Santana Series IV (later known as Santana 2.500) of 1987–94 (essentially Santana's version of the UK 90 and 110 range but still using leaf springs).

Santana formally ended its agreement with Land Rover in 1989, when the company became partially owned by Suzuki, but continued to develop its own range of vehicles, which remained visually similar to Land Rover's range. Licence-built Suzuki SJ models were also built at the plant, which was to be enlarged and adapted to Japanese production methods. At the time, it was expected that Suzuki would increase its holding of 18% in Santana and possibly take over the 31% then still held by the UK manufacturer. Until this time, the Santana models evolved and diverged from Land Rover's UK-manufactured vehicles. Santana models, for example, featured more ergonomic seats, disc brakes, turbo diesel engines and parabolic springs. In addition, the company manufactured a civilian version of its 88in Militar known as the Ligero that was unique to Santana; it was practically the same as the 88in Militar, available in a range of exclusive and bright colours to appeal to younger customers as a leisure vehicle. It had a canvas roof, although a fibreglass roof was an option, and a robust roll cage.

When Series IV Santana production ended, the jigs and production machinery were sold to Morattab in Iran, previously a customer for CKD Santana vehicles. Back in Europe, the lengthy evolution of Santana Land Rovers led to the development of the Santana PS10, a 109in in Station Wagon and commercial forms, production of which began in 2002. A final twist in the whole tale makes it a rarity now. In 2006, Iveco and Santana made an agreement that saw the advent of the Iveco Massif, a rebadged and restyled version of the Santana PS-10. It is believed that small sales of this machine led to the closure of the Linares plant in 2010 and with it, the demise of a vehicle with great potential.

Santana manufactured Series IIAs models until 1974 when it introduced its version of the Series III. The first Santana Series IIIs, like this one pictured, were made between 1974 and 1978 and were very similar to the Solihull-built models, although there were differences. As is evident here, the rear door and hinges and the wheel rims vary from the English components, and the vehicle has a Land Rover Santana badge on its rear panel.

Santana's version of the Series III did evolve slightly during its production run. As can be seen here, this LHD Station Wagon still bears a close resemblance to the Solihull models, but its driver and passenger door hinges are of a different design.

Santana's second version of the Series III was made between 1978 and 1983 and involved detail changes, as more components were made in Spain. This LHD vehicle looks like a Solihull Series III, but its roof panel and the door hinges are of a different design. The rear fixed side windows are also larger than those that would be found on UK-built models.

The Santana's redesigned roof panel was made from glass fibre rather than metal as used on English Series IIIs but fixed to the vehicle by being bolted to the windscreen and rear side panels in the same way.

Santana's next incarnation of the Series III was known as the Series IIIA (a designation not used in the UK) as the vehicle diverged further from the Solihull Land Rovers. The top of the bulkhead was redesigned to eliminate the bulkhead vents and facilitate fitting a larger one-piece windscreen in place of the two-piece version hitherto used.

The Series IIIA Santana featured a redesigned Land Rover Santana badge on its rear panel and side doors with one-piece wind-up windows, but despite the glass-fibre roof, the overall appearance was still very much Land Rover.

As seen on this 1984 88in model, the Series IIIA Santana featured air intake holes in the bonnet, which otherwise resembles the deluxe bonnet used on Series IIA and Series III Land Rovers in the UK. The plastic radiator grille was also now factory finished in black.

Later versions of the Santana Series IV became known as the Santana 2500, and production continued until 1994. This example that closely resembles a County Station Wagon has the 2500 designation incorporated into the pinstripes on the vehicle's side panels. The leaf springs are evident under the vehicle, and the wheels are Santana-made items.

The evolution of the Santana Series III 109in into the later variants followed the same progression as the 88in models, although there was a further version powered by an in-line six-cylinder engine of 3,429cc displacement offered with a choice of petrol or diesel fuel. The use of the six-cylinder required more room, hence the flush front panel on this 1982 model.

This 109in Santana truck-cab has all the features unique to Santana's Series IIIA and those unique to the six-cylinder models, namely the redesigned door hinges, wind-up door windows, one-piece windscreen and associated redesigned bulkhead as well as the flush front panel and vented deluxe bonnet.

Above left: The Series IIIA Santana featured these vents in the bonnet that acted as an air intake. Problems with water ingress led to them later being repositioned on the vehicle's wing.

Above right: The redesigned bulkhead has no bulkhead vents so is lower and facilitates the fitment of a, still hinged, larger one-piece windscreen. The redesigned door hinges are also clearly evident here.

Right: This Santana has unusual front hub ends that differ from UK-produced vehicles but were used across Santana's range. The slightly different wheel centre pressing can also be clearly seen here.

The bodywork of the five-door 109in Super Station Wagon is a curious mix of Series Land Rovers. Its glass-fibre roof, rear door, one-piece side doors and vented front wings are Santana parts, but the rear tub and side panels are like those of the Solihull-built Station Wagon.

The 109in Santana Series IV in its later 2500 DL form. Although it resembled a 110 Station Wagon, it was still reliant on leaf springs and would stay in production until 1994.

Santana exported its Land Rovers to parts of South America and North Africa during the 1960s. This truck-cab 109in is a 1978–83 model Santana Series III that was photographed in Morocco.

This multicoloured and sign written 109in model has been modified into a garage recovery truck. Both the modifications and the condition of the vehicle are testament to decades of hard work. Its parabolic leaf springs can be seen at the rear, and it has a tropical roof panel on its truck-cab roof.

The configuration of the much-used vehicle's dashboard illustrates the similarities and differences with the UK-built models. It resembles a Series IIA dash panel but is made from moulded plastic rather than metal.

Despite resembling a Series IIA dash panel, this LHD Santana 109in's dash panel is located in the position familiar to British Series III owners, in a binnacle in front of the driver.

Santana's 'Militar' Land Rovers were unique to Santana and built for the Spanish Army. The model was offered in both 88in and 109in wheelbase versions and did have similarities in appearance to the British Army's Half-Ton Lightweight models. A 109in version is pictured here. Later, a civilian derivative was offered and sold as the Ligero.

For a period, Series III Land Rovers were also assembled in the West African state of Angola during its time as a Portuguese colony. These were received from the UK as CKD kits and assembled by União Comercial de Automóveis, the local importer, at a plant near Luanda, Angola's capital city and a major seaport. The most visible detail that proves the origins of these vehicles is the special badge with the word 'UNIÃO' that was affixed under the standard Land Rover badge on the rear tub.

Chapter 5
Accessories

As with previous Series Land Rovers, the Series III could be equipped with additional equipment to make it suited to specific purposes. Its gearbox was suited to the fitting of a Power Take Off (PTO) that could provide drive to the rear for splined shafts to drive agricultural machinery and pumps, or to the front of the vehicle to drive equipment such as capstan and drum winches. In view of this, the factory approved a range of special equipment made by outside suppliers that had been evaluated prior to approval being granted. This included freewheeling hubs, winches, overdrives and towing equipment but also vehicle conversions such as the Searle of Sunbury on Thames, Carawagon camper conversions. The items were detailed in a loose-leaf folder that had a page per item and was divided into Land Rover, Range Rover and Special Equipment sections.

Freewheeling hubs, also known as locking hubs, deserve a few words of explanation. They have been in production for 4x4s since Arthur and Sadie Warn founded Warn Industries in 1948. It began with Warn's invention of wheel-locking hubs for adapting thousands of surplus World War Two Jeeps. It revolutionised the automotive industry, and, by 1954, Warn locking hubs were offered as optional factory equipment by major US automakers. The rest of the world soon followed, in particular, in the UK, Mayflower Auto Products – later Fairey – offered freewheeling hubs for Land Rovers that were factory-approved accessories. Freewheeling hubs are mechanical devices that disconnect the front wheels from the drive train of a part-time 4x4 system when four-wheel-drive is not required. The, once ubiquitous, freewheeling hubs seem to have become a bit controversial in recent years for various reasons including misinformation that abounds on online forums and the like. They do not engage four-wheel-drive; this is done in the transfer case. They do not lock the front diff, but they do engage and disengage the half-shaft from the hub of the wheel. When the hub is in the locked position, the shaft is engaged and when it is in the free position, it is disengaged. The intention of the hubs is to save fuel because, with the hubs in the free position and the Land Rover in 4x2, it takes less effort to move the vehicle because the front wheels are only being pushed along rather than the front prop and half-shafts. In theory, wear is decreased on the front axle's moving parts and tyres. It is here that some of the controversy arises, as many claim substantially improved fuel economy from the hubs, and others claim increased tyre life and reduced wear on the front axle and propshaft's moving parts. They also reduce the vibration that is transferred to the driver through the steering wheel. Their use requires remembering to engage them before going off-Tarmac, and they should be engaged from time to time to lubricate the moving parts adequately.

During the fifties, noted aviation company Fairey acquired Mayflower Automotive Products, including the factory in Tavistock, Devon, and with it the M.A.P. winches and freewheeling hubs for Land Rovers. The Fairey company dropped the M.A.P. hubs from production and offered a revised version of its own brand. Production of the noted Fairey overdrive ended during the eighties when new Land Rover products with permanent 4x4 made them largely superfluous and forced Fairey, latterly Fairey Winches and FW Winches Limited, to stop manufacture due to a lack of demand. The company, as a constituent part of the Fairey Group, went into liquidation in 1977. American company Superwinch bought the Tavistock works and continued making Fairey winches. The site was Superwinch's European base and manufacturing facility primarily dedicated to winch manufacture until it closed in 2019.

There was also a considerable variety of aftermarket items that were available for the Series III, ranging from freewheeling hubs and winches that hadn't been approved by Land Rover to items designed to make the vehicles more comfortable or more suited to specific roles including aftermarket windows and seats to convert utility hard-top models into something akin to a Station Wagon. Other accessories included aftermarket wheels of which the so-called 'eight-spokes', white steel wheels with eight spokes and triangular apertures were among the most common.

This 1982 109in Land Rover HCPU has been equipped with a Fairey mechanical PTO winch that was formerly used on a Yorkshire Electricity Board Land Rover. This mechanical drum winch is shaft driven by a PTO and can be used in working situations with the transfer box in neutral or in self-recovery situations with the transmission engaged. The golf ball on the handle is not original.

A popular accessory for Land Rovers of all types, especially in farming areas, was the Ifor Williams canopy for truck-cab models. Ifor Williams is a manufacturer of trailers and these canopies are from Cynwyd near Corwen in Denbighshire, North Wales. They are made from high-grade aluminium, for the framework and panels, and hot dip galvanized steel for the tailgate and hinges.

Freewheeling hubs have been made for numerous makes of 4x4 by a variety of manufacturers since the late 1940s. AVM was founded in 1957 in Brazil and has produced freewheeling hubs ever since. It has exported more than 80% of its production to countries around the globe. The company is based in premises in Cotia, greater São Paulo, Brazil. To engage or disengage these hubs, the centre portion is turned to where the 4x lines up with the four or the two to signify four- or two-wheel-drive.

Freewheeling hubs are mechanical devices that disconnect the front wheels from the drive train when four-wheel drive is not needed. This particular one was a sales aid or part of a counter display, as the hub has been neatly sectioned to display its internal workings. It is complete, right down to the sectioned hub gasket and so illustrates the workings of the freewheeling hub showing how 4x2 and 4x4 can still be engaged and how the splined internals move on each other.

By the 1970s, British Leyland was offering Fairey hubs for Land Rovers. They were of a slightly unusual design in that they relied on a plastic component, the so-called Spirolox ring, to hold the assembly together and permit engaging and disengaging as required. These aren't actually a ring; they resemble a cable tie and are held in place by a retaining spring. They can be troublesome and are easy to break, but spares are available. For the Series III there were two Fairey freewheeling hub kits – part numbers RTC 8021 and RTC 8022 – to account for the fact that the 109in Series III featured a 24-spline half-shaft where the freewheeling hub is positioned, whereas the 88ins had a 10-spline half-shaft. This is an RTC 8022 hub from a 1982 109in Series III. It is engaged and disengaged by turning the cover in the direction of the arrows.

This is a later-type Superwinch freewheeling hub installed on a Series III with 'Wolf' wheels that are from military Defenders and are currently a popular accessory for Series III Land Rovers. The Superwinch hub is engaged and disengaged by turning the centre bar in the same manner as the AVM units.

Power Train Products offered freewheeling hubs for Series III Land Rovers like the one seen here during a brake overhaul. These worked like other brands' hubs but, in reality, were rebranded Selectro hubs manufactured in Denver, Colorado, USA.

Although this Series III has been retrofitted with a late Series IIA wire grille, it wears a once popular accessory in the form of the radiator muff. These muffs enabled the engine to run warmer on winter days by reducing airflow to the vehicle's radiator.

Land Rovers, particularly those used for overland travel, were often fitted with a substantial roof rack to carry jerrycans, equipment and personal kit. One noted maker of such roof racks and access ladders for Series IIIs was Brownchurch, a company established in 1970. An indication of the capacity of the Brownchurch roof rack can be seen here where this 109in Station Wagon is loaded with two aluminium Grumman canoes.

The fitting of additional windows in hard-top Land Rovers has long been popular. This 1972 Series III probably started out as a hard-top but has been fitted with aftermarket Defender-style opening side windows to create a Station Wagon as well as Defender wheels and door mirrors.

This accessorised 88in Land Rover has been fitted with an additional side window in the form of a porthole from West Custom Windows of California. Such portholes were popular for custom van applications during the 1970s and 1980s, so it is appropriate for a 1973 Series III. This Land Rover has also been fitted with UK-made Weller eight-spoke custom wheels.

This petrol-engined 1982 88in Series III also has accessories typical of the era in which it was manufactured. Aside from the yellow paintwork, the Land Rover has chromed eight-spoke wheels, a variation on the 'white spokes' and a bull bar. In the UK, bull bars, sometimes known as 'bush bars' or 'roo bars', were a short-lived fashion inspired by Australian 4x4s where vehicles had such bars to prevent damage when in contact with cattle or kangaroos. Concerns about pedestrian safety led to their almost disappearing.

Chapter 6
Enthusiasts' Series IIIs

What constitutes an enthusiast's Series III is difficult to define in numerous ways because of the transition a Land Rover makes over the years from being brand new in a showroom to it becoming someone's cherished classic car. Series IIIs were produced from 1971 to the mid-1980s, so early examples were more than a decade old when newer ones were still to be sold for the first time. It's fair to assume that many gradually make a transition from being a new vehicle to being a used vehicle and pass through several owners' hands before some are purchased by owners who will do more than just maintain them and restore them or preserve them. Also, many working vehicles like utility Land Rovers were sold to commercial users who replaced their vehicles on a cyclical basis, meaning that for many years there was a plentiful supply of Series III Land Rovers available second-hand. The fact that the Series III is newer than its Series One and II/IIA predecessors means that it came to gain classic status later than them, and it can be argued that the arrival of second-hand coil spring Land Rovers hastened this. Over the last 20 years, the Series III has most definitely made the move from 'cheap second-hand Land Rover' to 'desirable classic', and this process has accelerated in the last decade. Evidence of this comes in the rising numbers of high-quality restorations, growing interest in the detail differences between the various models from different years of production and increasing numbers of Series IIIs at events for classic vehicles. The plentiful supply of Series IIIs meant that it was possible to get a bargain, unlike with some earlier models where prices have rocketed.

Another aspect of the age, cost and plentiful supply of Series III Land Rovers is that rather than simply restoring their Land Rovers, some enthusiasts modify them for off-road use, and some of the fashions and accessories once seen on earlier Series Land Rovers have had something of a renaissance within Series III circles, such as the fitting of aftermarket wheels and modern winches. It's fair to say that almost anything goes with Series IIIs.

This 1980 Series III 88in is essentially as the factory made it and is typical of many owned by Land Rover enthusiasts. It has been retrofitted with Defender-type door mirrors and radial tyres. It has a military canvas tilt fitted probably to replace the original as over the years the canvas degrades in sunlight and rain.

A Series III 88in hard-top with export windows and seats in the back is the ideal classic Land Rover for a family. This one has been fitted with a military-type front bumper, Defender door mirrors and aftermarket wheels with radial Mud Tyres (MT). It has the basic so-called razor edge bonnet, and its spare wheel is in the vehicle's loadspace.

Above and opposite above: This 1983 88in diesel Station Wagon has been modified for off-road use with the addition of a military front bumper, box section sill protectors, a snorkel for fording, LED headlamps and an LED light bar. Being a Station Wagon, it has a tropical roof panel and the deluxe bonnet with the rounded leading edge.

This 1984 2,286cc diesel County Station Wagon has had its Station Wagon roof and rear door assembly removed and replaced with an aftermarket tilt and aftermarket hood sticks. It also now has steel Weller eight-spoke wheels in place of the original rims. Fairey freewheeling hubs have also been fitted to the front axle.

The removal of the rear door has required the fitment of a tailgate and a still-camouflaged, ex-military one has been used. One thing that is standard is the position of the rear lights, as later-type Series IIIs had their stop and tail lights and indicators separated on the rear panels, unlike the earlier models where they were positioned next to each other. Later Series IIIs also had a rectangular rear fog light on the offside corner.

This 1972 88in has been rebuilt on a galvanized steel chassis and features an aftermarket tilt, door mirrors, reversing light and is fitted with 'modular' steel wheels and All Terrain (AT) tyres.

This 1982 88in hard-top has gained a few accessories to make it more practical for its owner. It has a front-mounted winch sheeted against the weather and aluminium chequer plate tread plates on the wing-tops to enable them to be stood on while accessing things carried in the Brownchurch roof rack. It also has chequer plate on the rear corners of the bodywork that can offer a degree of protection to the bodywork in off-road conditions.

This newly rebuilt Series III 88in has been assembled on a galvanized chassis and features a few subtle upgrades to make it suited to its owner's requirements. It has eight-spoke wheels that have been painted in a Limestone colour to resemble the original steel wheels. It has been fitted with a soft-top front seat-belt bar that provides somewhere at shoulder height to position the highest point of a three-point seat belt inside a canvas tilt.

This Portuguese-registered Series III has a slightly unusual export configuration roof: it has the double-skinned tropical roof panel affixed to hard-top sides fitted with 'export' fixed windows. It has been retrofitted with the steel wheels from the first generation of Land Rover Discovery, a popular upgrade, as it is a cheap way to get tubeless rims for a Series Land Rover.

A fashion that came to the fore soon after the advent of the redesigned Ninety and One Ten models was to fit aftermarket kits that gave the Series III the flush-fronted appearance of the newer models by fitting a new grille panel and bonnet. These components also proved useful when engine swaps were undertaken by providing more space for a repositioned radiator, so increasing room under the bonnet.

This 1972 Series III 88in, a utility hard-top in the popular Deep Bronze Green and Limestone colour scheme, is standard apart from its Defender wing mirrors and radial tyres. Its bodywork bears the scars of decades of hard work, which give it a charm of its own.

While the meaning of the rabbit toy on the radiator grille is unrecorded, a patinated Land Rover such as this 1972 88in, with a full tilt, a deluxe bonnet and its door tops removed in the sunshine, has a weather-beaten charm for summer motoring.

Another fashion that was popular for a number of years, before used, coil-sprung 90s were readily available second-hand, was to combine a Series III body with the mechanical components from a Range Rover. This, whether it used military Lightweight panels as here or the standard Series III, produced an exceptionally capable off-road machine because of its lightness of weight and small size. As a result, these machines, referred to as 'hybrids', were popular with Land Rover club members.

An ex-farm Series III 88in awaiting restoration by its enthusiast owner. Although it looks almost derelict, it is a vehicle with plenty of potential for restoration, as it is largely original, all its panels are present, and they are relatively undamaged. The growth of algae can be easily cleaned off and its front bumper replaced when the other work is carried out. It is likely to need some welding to its steel chassis and bulkhead because of its age.

A restoration project Series III offered for sale at a Land Rover enthusiasts' event and is seen here in the condition in which it was retired from farm use. The configuration of truck-cab and loadspace canopy was popular with farmers who carried their dogs or livestock in the back of the Land Rover, while Marine Blue was a popular colour for Series III Land Rovers.

This Portuguese-registered 109in Series III has been modified for off-road use with large MT tyres and a winch fitted in order to cope with extreme terrain. Inside its canvas tilt, it also has a roll bar fitted to protect the occupants in the event of the vehicle turning over.

This 1976 109in Series III has been modified with the fitting of a military-type front bumper that incorporates recovery eyes and the grille panel from an earlier Land Rover. The latter was a once popular way of getting extra lights on the front of a Land Rover in lieu of spot or fog lights, although this Land Rover also has a pair of rectangular aftermarket fog lights fitted. Its sills have been fitted with chequer plate sill protectors, and its cab has been fitted with an external sun visor.

This six-wheeled Land Rover is an unusual model in that it is a 6x6 conversion to a 1982 Stage One V8 by the Sandringham Motor Company, also known as Hotspur Cars. They were built to carry a payload of two tons. Some were sold to utility companies, used as load carriers, cherry pickers and the like by their commercial users. Land Rover's design brief was to use as many standard parts as possible, so the non-standard Series III parts are the centre axle and prop shafts. This example has been upgraded with modern Defender grille and headlight surrounds, wheel arches and unusual wheel trims.

This six-wheeled Land Rover has also been fitted with numerous later model components, including Defender front wings, bonnet and military Wolf wheels. It also appears to have Defender axles, which suggest it uses Land Rover's post-Series III permanent four-wheel-drive system and so has freewheeling hubs on its rear axle to enable it to run as a 6x4 and prevent wind-up between the two rear axles.

An English take on the popular Australian 'tray back' pick-up is this modified 109in chassis-cab, with an especially constructed rear load bed that has been additionally fitted with an Ifor Williams canopy. Military Defender Wolf rims have been fitted with military 'bar grip' tyres, and the bespoke machine looks ready for hard work.

Land Rovers, regardless of their wheelbase, lend themselves to being used stripped to the body cappings with the windscreen folded forward onto the bonnet's spare-wheel mount. This Portuguese-registered, left-hand-drive model, in an unusual shade of red, looks ready for going to the beach.

This LHD 109in is also Portuguese-registered and has been tastefully upgraded internally with seat-belt bars and high-back driver and passenger seats. Externally, the Land Rover is standard, but its full-tilt configuration is more commonly found on military 109in Land Rovers than civilian models.

Chapter 7
Land Rover Clubs

There is a longstanding tradition of Land Rover clubs in the UK and beyond that reaches back to the 1950s when, in conjunction with the Rover Company, the Land Rover Owners' Club (LROC) was formed. The organisation was owned by the Rover Company and its central office was based at the Solihull factory. While the company funded and staffed the organisation, numerous geographically separate area branches were set up. All members received a magazine entitled *Land Rover Review* on a quarterly basis. Things took a step forward in 1966 when the Rover Company revised the club structure. The branches of the LROC were asked to rename as Rover Owners' Clubs and affiliate to a new body called the Rover Owners Association (ROA). The Rover Company still funded the revised organisation and each year the ROA (Headquarters Club) organised the National Rally open to all ROA members. The quarterly publication was then titled *Rover Review*.

Things changed again in 1978, midway through Series III production, when the Association of Rover Clubs (ARC) was established to supersede the ROA because British Leyland now owned Rover and withdrew from club organisation. At its inception, most Land Rover clubs were area based, but recent decades have seen increasing numbers of model specific Land Rover clubs established. In 2006, the ARC became the Association of Land Rover Clubs (ALRC), and in 2016 the ALRC comprised around 37 UK-based member clubs and ten overseas clubs. The tradition of the National Rally has endured; in 1978, it was held at Heath and Reach, Bedfordshire and hosted by Anglian ROC. In 1988, as 40 years of Land Rover were being marked, the rally took place at Trentham Gardens, Staffordshire, hosted by Staffs and Shrops LRC. By the time the 50th anniversary came around in 1998, the National Rally was held at Eastnor Park, Herefordshire and hosted by the ARC and Midland ROC. In 2006, after the ARC became the ALRC, the National Rally was held at Manby near Louth, Lincolnshire and co-hosted by Lincolnshire and the Staffordshire and Shropshire LRC. The 2008 National Rally marking 60 years of Land Rover was back at Eastnor Park, Herefordshire and again hosted by Midland ROC.

In parallel to this 'official' sequence of events, other clubs were formed, notably the All Wheel Drive Club that was formed in 1968 and thrives to this day. Other all-makes clubs followed, so by the time the Series III was in production, there was an active club scene for those who wanted to drive their vehicles off-road for recreational purposes. These clubs tended to organise off-road competitions, greenlaning (as the driving of unsurfaced minor roads is referred to in the UK) and social activities. In recent years, other clubs have been established to cater for the owners of classic Land Rovers and specific models of Land Rover. These clubs' events reflect this, as they undertake activities more akin to those of classic car clubs, although greenlaning and motorsport trials remain popular. These clubs often include attendance at vintage rallies and steam fairs where, increasingly, an exhibition class for classic Land Rovers is to be found.

4x4 trials involve drivers negotiating a difficult stretch of ground without hitting any of the 12 pairs of canes 'gates' that determine a section. Hitting a cane gets a driver the number of points on that cane, and the gates start at 12 and successively number down to 1; fewest penalty points wins. This Series III driver is negotiating canes on a side-slope. The canes are placed far enough apart for the vehicles to pass between them, and the skill comes in traversing the uneven ground without becoming stuck and exiting each gate in the right place to access the next one, so knowing when and where to turn for example.

The type of trials and terrain varies depending on the geography and geology of the venue. This Portuguese Series III is being driven on dry, rocky ground, while Wales in winter, for example, can be considerably wetter and muddier. Each type of terrain offers its own challenges.

Greenlaning involves driving on unsurfaced minor rights of way, which tend to be in rural areas. These Series IIIs are seen on a famous green lane in Mid Wales known as Strata Florida (Ystrad Fflur), Latin for 'Vale of Flowers', that was once the route used by monks to access the abbey of Strata Florida in the 13th century.

Many old packhorse bridges on green lanes are not wide enough for vehicles so drivers often rely on a ford next to them. Wise drivers check the depth of water in fords before driving into the water, although on this occasion the water isn't deep enough to be a problem for this 1982 Santana 109in Series III.

Steam rallies and vintage vehicle rallies generally welcome Series III Land Rovers as bona fide classics now. This 1972 Series III Land Rover is displayed with another, once ubiquitous, sight on British farms, a Ferguson tractor generally known as the 'grey Fergy'.

This 1974 109in Station Wagon is parading in the ring at the famous Masham Steam Engine and Fair Organ Rally that has been an annual event near the North Yorkshire town of Masham for more than half a century.

This row of Marine Blue 88in Series IIIs are on display at a relatively new but increasingly popular event for leaf spring Land Rovers, namely 'Leafers at t'Pit'. The event is so named because, since its inception, it has taken place at venues connected with the UK's mining heritage.

This trio of Series III Station Wagons, two 88ins and a 109in (left), are gathered in the central arena of the once famous Land Rover show at Billing Aquadrome in Northamptonshire where one of the attractions was club parades such as this.

Other Land Rover club activities are lower key. This is a Sunday lunchtime gathering of enthusiasts at a scenic West Yorkshire pub where the 1980 Series III 109in (left) is in company with two Series IIA predecessors.

The Ex-Military Land Rover Association is one Land Rover club aimed at a specific type of Land Rover owner and that has numerous Series III owners within its ranks because the British military used so many Series III Half-Ton and 109in models and also had a number of CL 88ins.

The Land Rover Lightweight Club, for owners of the military Lightweight or Half-Ton Land Rovers, regularly stages displays of its vehicles that include restored and 'civilianised' examples of the distinctive Lightweight. This display is at the annual Billing Land Rover Show.

The famous Camel Trophy expeditions only used Series III Land Rovers on one occasion; the 1983 Zaire (Democratic Republic of the Congo) event that travelled from Kinshasa to Kisangani using 88in and 109in Station Wagons. There was a Portuguese team in the event, which is why this enthusiast has built a 1983 event tribute vehicle.

There is no reason why well-maintained Series III Land Rovers are not capable of lengthy journeys, so groups of club members or friends often undertake extended holiday trips. This 109in Station Wagon, known as 'The Marrakech Express', was prepared for an overland trip to Morocco as recently as 2015. It was driven from England to Marrakech and spent a couple of months touring the country before being driven back across Europe to England. This photo shows it at Tamegroute in the Draa River valley of southern Morocco on the northern edge of the Sahara Desert.

Further reading from

As Europe's largest transport publisher, we also produce a wide range of magazines

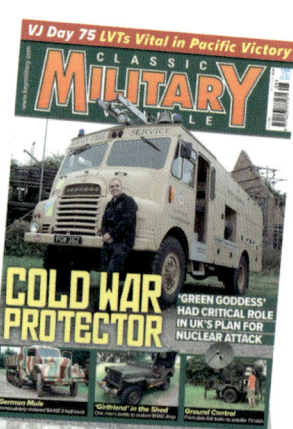

Visit: shop.keypublishing.com for more details